CAPTURING JOY

※ The Story of Maud Lewis ※

Jo Ellen Bogart ※ Illustrated by Mark Lang

Tundra Books

Text copyright © 2002 by Jo Ellen Bogart
Illustrations copyright © 2002 by Mark Lang
Maud Lewis art copyright © 2002 by the Art Gallery of Nova Scotia

The publisher extends sincere appreciation to the Art Gallery of Nova Scotia for permission
to reproduce the paintings of Maud Lewis. The paintings were photographed by Don Stanfield
and the late Bob Brooks.

Published in Canada by Tundra Books,
481 University Avenue, Toronto, Ontario M5G 2E9

Published in the United States by Tundra Books of Northern New York,
P.O. Box 1030, Plattsburgh, New York 12901

Library of Congress Control Number: 2001095372

National Library of Canada Cataloguing in Publication Data

Bogart, Jo Ellen, 1945-
Capturing joy : the story of Maud Lewis

ISBN 0-88776-568-8

1. Lewis, Maud, 1907-1970. 2. Painters–Nova Scotia–Biography. I. Lang, Mark. II. Title.

ND249.L447B63 2002   759.11   C2001-902804-0

We acknowledge the support of the Canada Council for the Arts and
the Ontario Arts Council for our publishing program.

We acknowledge the financial support of the Government of Canada through the
Book Publishing Industry Development Program for our publishing activities.

Design: Blaine Herrmann

Printed in Hong Kong

1 2 3 4 5 6   07 06 05 04 03 02

A small figure moved through the crisp snow of a January evening. She knocked on the door of the tiny house by the highway where Everett Lewis, the fish peddler, lived. Everett had advertised for a housekeeper, but Maud Dowley knew that the lonely man needed a wife and companion. She knew that she should be that wife.

It was not long before Maud married Everett and moved in to share his life. She accepted that it would not be a life of luxury. The house had just one small room, with a sleeping loft above. There was no indoor plumbing or electricity, and hardly room to turn around.

Maud began to do the cooking and housework, but it was hard for her. She was not strong because her shoulders were hunched from birth defects and her hands crippled from arthritis.

As time passed, Everett went back to doing most of the housework, as he had done for years. Maud went back to an activity she loved – painting.

As a child, she had painted Christmas cards with her mother, Agnes, in a comfortable house in South Ohio, Nova Scotia, where Maud had been born. Her mother's family had always had artistic ability, and Agnes encouraged her daughter to develop her talents. Little Maud had played the piano until her hands became too misshapen to manage the keys. Fortunately, her disability didn't keep her from holding a paintbrush.

In her new home, Maud began to paint Christmas cards again, selling them for a nickel, often to Everett's customers on his fish-peddling route. The Christmas cards had scenes of sleepy villages under falling snow, whirling skaters on a frozen pond, bluebirds surprised by an early snowfall, or a single horse pulling a sleigh.

BLUE BIRDS IN SNOW

When she moved on to larger paintings, Everett used his scrounging talents to get materials for Maud's work. He found discarded cans of paint from fishing boats and scraped off the dried layer to reveal good paint beneath. He cut uneven panels from cast-off scraps of wood and cardboard for her to paint on. With a metal TV tray as her easel and her paints squeezed into sardine cans, Maud painted for hours straight, supporting her painting hand with the other.

Sitting in the corner by the house's one window, Maud began to create scenes from the early years of her life. Though her frail health had hurt her school attendance, Maud's paintings often showed children heading to school or on the school playground. Bright colors and outstretched arms tell of active, happy children. Maud's joyful memories of school in South Ohio remained in spite of the cruel teasing she suffered after the family's move to the coastal town of Yarmouth.

Children to School

M aud's father, Jack Dowley, had been a blacksmith and harness maker. She remembered watching as he lovingly fashioned the leather harnesses for the oxen, each one different and perfectly fitted. Maud painted images of oxen with sweet faces and comical eyelashes, wearing beautiful yokes and harnesses with bells.

OXEN IN WINTER

Maud had a love of animals and her family always had a cat. Bright-eyed kittens grew from her brushes, usually surrounded by flowers and butterflies. Her farm scenes, with horses and chickens, showed gentle people caring for the animals. Maud also painted wildlife, like a mother deer with her fawn before a lake at sunset.

Maud's married life still included animals. Poor as they were, she and Everett always had pets around the house.

Three Black Cats

As a child, Maud and her family enjoyed daylong outings in a fringe-topped horse and buggy. How happy these outings must have been, with fresh air, the sound of the horse's hooves, and laughter. Maud painted many scenes of people out for a ride.

Horse-drawn Carriage with Dog

After leaving school at the age of fourteen, Maud led a quiet life, tucked away in her parents' house in Yarmouth. She might have expected to go on living with her mother and father as they grew old. However, in her early thirties, she suffered the loss of both her parents within two years. She managed to stay on in the house with her older brother, Charles, for a while, but he soon sent her to live with their mother's sister, Ida Germaine. Charles went away to war and, though he survived, he never saw his sister again.

Aunt Ida, a kind woman, lived in a well-kept home up the coast in Digby, Nova Scotia. It was here that Maud observed the seaside life that would appear in so much of her work. Maud's paintings were filled with boats, docks, lighthouses, seagulls, lovely shoreline hills, and people working at the fishing trade. From Digby, it was just a few miles to the Marshalltown home she would later share with Everett Lewis.

Portrait of Eddie Barnes and Ed Murphy, Lobster Fishermen, Bay View, Nova Scotia

A nother subject of Maud's paintings was the old Model T car that Everett had owned when they married. The car gave Maud freedom as she went with Everett on his fish-peddling route. Her paintings show the couple traveling the roads of beautiful Nova Scotia throughout the seasons.

MODEL T ON TOUR

Maud often showed her husband, Everett, in her paintings. The man that Maud spent half of her life with was known to be difficult and miserly. Everett had suffered a hard childhood, living in poverty with his mother after his father left. Mother and son spent years at the Poor Farm on the Marshalltown highway, next to where Everett later placed the little house he bought. The young Everett worked for his keep, staying with different families, and sometimes he did not have enough to eat.

As an adult, Everett was good at making do with what he could find for free, hating to spend money. He was so afraid of being poor again that he would not buy the simple things that would have made their lives more comfortable. A few good friends looked out for Maud, so she would not suffer too much from Everett's stinginess. Still, Maud included her husband in many paintings, with his lanky frame and red hat, showing him as a capable and hardworking man.

Horses Hauling Logs in Winter

M aud had her own way of depicting the world. She never painted shadows on the bare ground in scenes of summer or fall. Only in snow did Maud create depth with soft blue shadows.

In her water scenes, Maud revealed a wonderful sense of light and dark. Sunlight glowed on the sea's blue horizon and the hills threw dark shadows on the water. Boats flashed bright reflections of their sides, while their masts and the wharf poles became wavering images in the moving water.

CAPE ISLANDER

S| ome of Maud's paintings show scenes that very rarely, or never, really happen. Brightly colored autumn leaves in snow can be explained as a very early snow-fall. What is the explanation for fluffy pink blossoms on evergreen trees? Maud had her own vision of beauty.

Cows Grazing Among Flowering Spruces

Many of Maud's winter landscapes show snow in the foreground, while faraway mountains are painted green. It is more likely that the mountains would be snow-covered, high above a warmer valley, but the effect is lovely to behold.

Covered Bridge with Skaters

After Everett sold the Model T, Maud seldom left the little house. She seemed content to watch the world pass by on the highway that ran just a stone's throw from her door.

While Maud was creating her paintings to sell, she was also turning the little house into a work of art. She painted the stairs to the sleeping loft, the stacked bread boxes where they stored their food, the walls, and even the woodstove. Bright flowers, birds, and butterflies brightened the front door and tulips adorned the window glass.

Maud Lewis did not seek fame, but word of her charming paintings spread far from her Nova Scotia home. Travelers began to stop and buy paintings from the cheerful, but painfully shy, artist. So many people wanted paintings that they often bought works that were barely finished and still wet. After a while, visitors to the area made a point of going to Marshalltown to see Maud and buy her paintings. Local residents were surprised to see famous people making the trip to the little painted house.

Maud gained much attention from newspaper and magazine articles written about her and from a television program. The number of requests for paintings got larger and larger, until Maud had trouble keeping up. Migraine headaches, made worse by paint and woodstove fumes and perhaps by her own cigarette smoking, slowed her down and Everett sometimes picked up a brush to help. When Maud was sixty-seven, her health failed. She died in 1970.

Maud Lewis was buried in a cemetery near her home. Many people came to say good-bye to the tiny woman whose paintings had brought them so much enjoyment. Since then, she has become one of Canada's best-known and best-loved folk artists. The joy that she captured in every painting lives on.

Afterword

Maud Kathleen Dowley was born on March 7, 1903 in
South Ohio, Nova Scotia, Canada and died in Digby General
Hospital on July 30, 1970. Her husband of thirty-two years,
Everett Lewis, continued to live in the painted house until
his death nine years later. Many people thought it was
very important that the little house be preserved for
future generations. They formed a group called the
Maude Lewis Painted House Society (Maud with an "e")
and worked towards having the little house saved.
As time passed, the house became more and more
dilapidated. Finally, in 1984, the province of
Nova Scotia bought the house on behalf of the
Art Gallery of Nova Scotia and put it into safe storage.
Extensive conservation was carried out on all parts of
the house, including Maud's many hand-painted
decorations. Every effort was made to preserve the
setting as it had been. Maud and Everett's little house,
including some of their possessions, now occupies
gallery space, along with many of Maud's paintings,
in the Art Gallery of Nova Scotia at
1723 Hollis St. in Halifax, Nova Scotia.

WISHING WELL AND FLOWERS

FOUNTAIN AND BIRDS